Cate

and their Cocoons

by Margaret Gallo

Harcourt
SCHOOL PUBLISHERS

Cover, ©Corel; p.3, (tr) ©Tim Laman/National Geographic Image Collection, (tl) (br) ©John Foxx/ ImageState Stock Photography, (bl) (bc) ©Corbis; p.4, ©MICHAEL & PATRICIA FOGDEN/Minden Pictures; p.5, ©J.A.L. Cooke/OSF/Animals Animals; p.6, (t) ©Corbis, (b) ©Corel; p.8, ©Photodisc; p.9, ©Donald Specker/Animals Animals; p.10, ©Richard Kolar/Animals Animals; p.10-11, (c) ©James H. Carmichael/Photo Researchers, Inc.; p.11, ©Hans Pfletschinger/Peter Arnold, Inc.; p.12, ©Patti Murray/Animals Animals; p.13, ©Dwight Kuhn; p.14, (l) ©E.R. Degginger/Animals Animals, (c) ©MICHAEL DURHAM/Minden Pictures, (r) ©Ralph Reinhold/Animals Animals.

Printed in the United States of America

ISBN 10: 0-15-350504-4
ISBN 13: 978-0-15-350504-1

Ordering Options
ISBN 10: 0-15-350333-5 (Grade 3 Below-Level Collection)
ISBN 13: 978-0-15-350333-7 (Grade 3 Below-Level Collection)
ISBN 10: 0-15-357492-5 (package of 5)
ISBN 13: 978-0-15-357492-4 (package of 5)

1 2 3 4 5 6 7 8 9 10 179 12 11 10 09 08 07 06

Butterflies flutter among flowers during the day. Moths fly to porch lights at night. Butterflies have brightly colored wings. Moths have darker, softer colors. Butterflies and moths do not start out that way. In fact, they don't even start their lives with wings!

Butterflies and moths are insects. They start out as eggs. A female moth or butterfly will lay thousands of eggs on the leaves of plants. The eggs are very tiny. Some of the eggs hatch. Other eggs might get eaten by insects or animals that prey on insect eggs.

When the eggs hatch, the tiny caterpillars bite their way out of the eggshell. That is their first meal. Then they eat the leaf of the plant. The tiny caterpillars are called larvae. Tiny caterpillars spend most of their time eating, and soon they start to grow.

All caterpillars are not the same. There are thousands of different kinds of caterpillars. Many caterpillars are about the size of a paper clip. Others can be very tiny, and some can be very large and long. Some caterpillars are fuzzy. Others are smooth.

All caterpillars have the same body parts. Their bodies are made up of thirteen parts, called segments. The first three segments have pairs of legs with claws on the end. The rest of the segments have legs with hooks on them. These hooks help the caterpillar cling to a leaf.

Tent caterpillars work in social groups. They spin large webs of silk in apple or cherry trees. Hundreds of them will spin a "tent" where several branches meet. When they leave the tent to eat, the caterpillars leave a shallow trail of silk to follow back home.

When a caterpillar grows big enough, it sheds its skin. To do this, the caterpillar spins a spiral of silk. It holds onto the silk so that it does not fall and creeps forward. As it does this, it leaves its old skin behind. Then the caterpillar starts to grow again.

Every time a caterpillar grows, it sheds its skin. Soon the caterpillar is ready for the next stage of life. Some caterpillars will grow into butterflies. If the caterpillar is to become a butterfly, it forms a hard covering called a chrysalis over its whole body.

Other caterpillars turn into moths. These caterpillars spin a cocoon. First, the caterpillar attaches itself to a leaf. Then, it reels out a strand of silk. Soon, strands of silk cover its body. Sometimes, the caterpillar weaves bits of leaves into the cocoon. That helps hide the cocoon.

Inside the cocoon, the caterpillar's body changes. A caterpillar may stay inside a cocoon for several days. Others may stay inside for a whole winter! This time is dangerous for the caterpillar because some animals like to eat cocoons.

One day the caterpillar is ready to come out of the cocoon. Its body has changed into a moth. The cocoon has become very thin. You can see the moth inside. The moth breaks free and wiggles out of the cocoon. Before long it is ready to fly away.

The same body changes take place inside a chrysalis. The caterpillar will turn into a beautiful butterfly. When the butterfly is ready, it breaks free.

The butterflies and moths wait for their wings to dry. Then they fly away to lay eggs. Soon the life cycle starts all over again.

Think Critically

1. What is the first stage of a butterfly or moth's life?

2. What body parts do all caterpillars have?

3. Why might a caterpillar's cocoon not make it through a long winter?

4. How are a chrysalis and a cocoon alike? How are they different?

5. How can you tell this story is nonfiction?

Science

Draw a Picture Think about the stages of a butterfly's or a moth's life. Divide a piece of paper into four parts. Draw pictures to show how the moth or butterfly changes over time.

School-Home Connection Explain to a family member how a caterpillar makes its cocoon. Talk about when you have seen butterflies and moths.

Word Count: 567 (576)